Unfinished Portrait

POEMS BY
Luivette
Resto

TIA CHUCHA PRESS
LOS ANGELES

Printed in the United States of America
ISBN 978-1-882688-36-4

Book Design: Jane Brunette
Cover Art: *Afro-Cuban* by Yasmin Hernandez

PUBLISHED BY:
Tia Chucha Press
A Project of Tia Chucha's Centro Cultural, Inc.
PO Box 328
San Fernando, CA 91341
www.tiachucha.com

DISTRIBUTED BY:
Northwestern University Press
Chicago Distribution Center
11030 South Langley Avenue
Chicago, IL 60628

*Tia Chucha Press is the publishing wing of Tia Chucha's Centro Cultural, Inc., a 501 (c) 3
nonprofit corporation. Tia Chucha's Centro Cultural has received funding from the National
Endowment for the Arts, the California Arts Council, Los Angeles County Arts Commission,
Los Angeles Department of Cultural Affairs, Los Angeles Community Redevelopment Agency,
Thrill Hill Foundation, the Center for Cultural Innovation, the Middleton Foundation, the Panta
Rhea Foundation, the Attias Family Foundation, Not Just Us Foundation, the Liberty Hill
Foundation, Youth Can Service, Toyota Sales, Solidago Foundation, and other grants as well as
donations from Bruce Springsteen, John Densmore, Lou Adler, Richard Foos, Adrienne Rich,
Tom Hayden, Dave Marsh, Denise Chávez and John Randall of the Border Book Festival,
Luis & Trini Rodríguez, among others.*

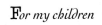

For my children

Table of Contents

The White Girl in Her

Because the accent does not match the skin,
all her friends think she was hatched
or fell on her head when she came off the plane.
Others say it is the white girl in her.

She is supposed to have trouble
with common American phrases,
pronounce "this" like "deece"
translate Spanish to English with ease
for the new mainlanders,
work with the underprivileged,
hate the white oppressor,
own records by Ricky Martin.

Instead the white girl
makes her listen to Tony Bennett,
dancing to whatever the radio plays.
The white girl got her into Cornell
and helped her in boarding school,
gave her knowledge of Europe,
stole her accent and
replaced it with one from the Valley.

It is the white girl that makes her that way,
the city whispers.

The girl with the curly hair and
dark circles around her eyes
stares at her friends and family
gathering around her with the Santero,
the Puerto Rican flag, César Chávez's picture,
homemade rice and beans, and booming congas
as they await for the Latin exorcism to begin.

Dancing Might Make Her Go Away

Names change history.
The hue lightens,
dims with each question.

Because loved ones encourage
the white girl to come out,
entertain island relatives with annunciations.
She repossesses the larynx, alter surnames,
erases 100 years of history.

Because job interviews are unlike game shows
and my name is hard to understand
beneath a blanket of accents.

Conversations about "keeping it real"
echo childhood memories on Adams Avenue.
"Never forget where you come from
cuz you'll be back with all those books."
Coconut, oreo, vendapatria
erode the brain with guilt and doubt
while dictionary pages turn under flashlights.
Dreams of self-advancement rise
like the flour tortillas
great-grandma Valencia made.

Because the white girl is treated like a light switch
off and on
on and off
with inevitable fear of turning her
on and on and on.

Where is the candle wax on wooden floors,
santeros covered in white with yellow beads around their necks
chanting Spanish words.
Where are the booming congas and tambourines,
because dancing might make her go away.

Questions for the Young Woman Representing Latinos, Women, Puerto Ricans, and People of Color

I wonder why
in a room full of white intellectuals
when the topic becomes
immigration, diversity in our schools,
multiculturalism, the end of affirmative action,
bilingual education, racial profiling,
women in the senate, they ask me
do I eat California table grapes,
how do I pronounce my name,
why the Spanish alphabet has 30 letters,
when are the peak travel times in Puerto Rico,
do I know María Rodriguez from The Bronx,
how do I roll my "r's," how good are my translation skills,
when did I come to America,
was it hard getting a green card,
when did I learn to speak English,
can I teach them a new phrase
to impress their maid.
Why is that all eyes fall on me
waiting for an answer to their questions.

Guazabara

Doubters already exist
because they believe I am a phase in your life
that will dim like the sun at dusk.

They are wrong. They are wrong.
Words gravitate towards me because
I give birth to the poetry you claim.

You are the investment that never flourished
not me, who chases villanelles through corn fields.

You hide your accent from people,
not me: I defiantly speak in different tongues,
confusing, enraging others.

You are the token they use in statistics and diversity charts,
and me, the mistake they never made again.

You are quiet, lonely, insecure,
scared of rejection,
not me: the guazabara, the warrior,
blowing smoke rings out of my mouth with a devilish smile.

Others may control your divinity and inner-truths,
but I untie strings from my feet and wrists,
never believing in the alleged words of men.

You are the barren mother who rubs her uterus at least once a day
not me: I awaken every morning with children tickling my feet.

When acceptance and certainty come looking for you,
you will hear my battle cry through the fields,
as I swing my club ululating for your salvation.

Tattoos

Caridad loves tattoos.
For her, the body is both
machine and portable museum.
Daily, she admires the portraits needled into
her imperfect body.

Swirls of red and ovals of black
cross her flesh,
the Taino symbol for hurricane
on her right shoulder blade.
Hypnotizing onlookers.
The Taina fertility goddess Atabey
painted on her stomach,
smiles down on her uterus.

The first tattoo is her favorite,
on her lower back
left of her spine.
There they stood,
two flags of Mexico and Puerto Rico.
Waving in the stillest weather
of her brown flesh.

People ask Caridad
what her flags mean.
A man, cultural identity, stupidity?
Many wonder, no one guesses right.
Busy gossips never think of the child

she hid from conversations.
He would have been beautiful,
have her eyes.
With each passing year,
her tattoos became badges of him.

She carried him every day
talking, teaching him:
the purpose and place of accents,
where the moon lives in the day,
how the rustling of trees sound
like waves on the shores of Puerto Rico.

All the mothers laugh at her,
calling her the colorful talking loca
as she continues to add more pictures
to her body for her child's company.

Nightly Prayer to the Unborn Child

Sacrificial children only exist
in fables or Bible stories.
Do you forgive me
or hate me for living without you?

What do you see from your new home?
Do you live in Heaven or Hell?
Dream of our fantastical life?
Tickling each other
until one of us burps.

I feel your hair
between my fingers
and the emptiness of each reason.

I remember
hoping for a miscarriage,
denying your sanctity
so guilt would disappear.

Pangs filled my womb
as I went to penance that day.
I curse myself for fucking,
Fuck god for existing.

Celebrate you eternally.

Notes on Anonymity

With a butterfly on her hip bone
he draws her pronounced curves
in the sand using all of his fingertips
capturing the obsidian smoothness of her torso.

She paints imaginary tollbooths on his nipples
stopping his lips each time they believe in affection.
Her cheeks travel up and down his back
savoring his skin.

They tease one another with
dreams of fictional children chasing seagulls in May
as the ocean awakens them
between kisses and fistfuls of wet sand tossed
just to see the other one dirty.

An April Kiss

That evening when your mouth touched mine
underneath the imaginary guava tree,

I prayed for the separation of reality and fiction.
Standing in a timeless vacuum, our eyes closed

creating a universe minus memories of
slammed doors, holy promises,
old photographs curling on firewood

as nectar dripped down my neck.

A Feminine Agreement

It was a contracted agreement,
we wanted to do what others lie about.

But the evening became next week's morning
with your hair on my chest and
my hand on your fertility arch.

You didn't say much as I kissed your thighs
and told you about those fantasies.
You moaned yes as I touched you
where calloused, unmanicured hands had been.

My heart paused as you tilted your head.
Lips thinner than Bible pages
but no matter.

You murmured how you could not stay any longer.
We repeated goodbyes
as you kept forgetting
silver barrettes on the dresser.
We wrote love letters
Rehashing the caress and hum of each other's touch.
But daily affirmations collapsed
into monthly updates
with no more mention of our sinful evening.

You connected with someone else.
I forget his name
as I lie next to my lover wishing his
hair was yours.

Soledad's Sexual Experiment

That evening
her hands became explorers
moving from her breasts,
palming a smooth stomach,
running an outline around the
fish shaped beauty mark above her bellybutton.

Soledad gazed between her thighs
allowing her fingertips to overflow her body,
as she recited
the Book of Genesis.

Faded Lipsticks

Fortune must be a man because
it comes only once.
God must be a man,
who else could be so incomprehensible,
so magnetic.

Morning never sets on the wounded,
breathes life into a perilous lung
seeking salvation with every exile.
Mistakes feel permanent,
blood stains, nail polish, death.

Constellations gather around dreams
of lovely girls asking for more, more, more.
Dreams exist in slums, pink filled bedrooms, padded walls,
in the jean pockets of teenagers, the backseats of mustangs,
newspaper clippings, operating rooms,
prison cells, church doorsteps,
in this year's harvest.

The right kiss on the mouth,
unsure whose heart beats fervently,
soothes the epidermis,
tingles tips of toes,
makes the heart salsa to its favorite song,
makes you want more
with the wetness of each tongue stroke,
smell perfection with each breath of his scent.

In the Beginning

This poem began seven years ago in Olin Library
between *I am Joaquín* and *Lost Among the Found*.
You asked me philosophical questions filled with idealism,
"What do you want? What makes you happy?"

Laughter and silence were my responses
as Shakespearean theories of perversion and morality
reminded me of my initial scholastic mission.

Soft brown eyes of expectation for a better life.

Skipping through the S's
I thought about your question
as my fingers dusted off your poem.
My feet felt the cracks of the 1970 tile
and the cold indifference of thirty year old marble.

The ground was mine.

My wants and happiness seemed selfish
when I represented generations
who looked at me as an investment
waiting for the stock to rise so they can cash out.
A ticker wrapped around my head.
My diploma was their diploma.

Lost in a world of confusion.

Sonnets are my favorites, I told you.
They epitomize the definition of love.
Neruda did it best.
Promise you will write me one some day,
you asked.

Only poets write those things, I answered,
and they became extinct with the dinosaurs.
Sonnets and odes do not pay the bills
my grandmother's ghost reminds me.

My odds are great but my spirit is strong.

Then you will write me one,
you declare.
Only if I can I call you Neftalí tonight?
I mouthed.

Sonnet for José's Enchiladas

Every spring you grant me the honor of your enchiladas.
You advise me it's a process and my impatience is unnecessary.

My mind rewinds to our first meal.
I despised your reputation and nicknamed you Lech.
But by dessert I adored your ambition
when you told me you changed your name
with hopes of forgetting an unapologetic father.
"I named myself after the Aztec god who created it all
and Zapata who fought for the rights of my people but
I kept my first name for the consideration of friends and family."
I had never met anyone, besides me, who had a harder time
  explaining their name.
He was it. We were destined to plant our own tree.

The smell of your enchiladas awaken me to the present
as you feed me a slice of cheddar cheese letting your fingers
  glide across my chin.

Ode to Cuchifrito

Ahh!
When my stomach grumbles
and my wallet can only hold a $5 bill,
my brown eyes gravitate to the first set
of hot light bulbs by a foggy window.

Oh cuchifrito stand what would I do
without your relleno de papa
deep fried in Mazola oil
and stuffed with my choice of
hot ham and cheese or ground beef?

But what of the alcapurrias?
my stomach asks,
made with yucca giving them a bright orange hue.
Or alcapurrias made with platanos and guineos?

You forgot the pastelillos
my palate reminds me:
Round orange disks flattened with a rolling pin,
stuffed with beef or guava with cheese,
then closed and joined by the intricate technology of a fork.

Oh cuchifrito!

Loose Tongue

On the fourth morning of January
my tongue seceded from my mouth.

Burned by words
like "spic" and "wetback"
occupying its palatable home;
mistreated like vecina Candela
the evenings she undercooks the rice.
Spanish words raided
with forced entrance of vosotros.

Puerto Ricans
sped through its taste buds,
masked as Europeans
with pointy iron hats and stiff moustaches,
screaming,
"Conquistador!"

As I chased it across opened photo albums,
newspapers, love letters,
my tongue reminded me of
conversations spoken once a year
when it took control
with words like "el building" and "bodega."

My tongue wanted a new home.

It chanted for the spirits of Pedro Albizu Campos
and my great-grandmother Tula
to possess my body
as I fell to catch my tongue between my brown fingers.

Translator

Hadley, Massachusetts 2003

I sat at the Registry of Motor Vehicles
when three men no taller than five feet walked in,
question marks spreading on their faces
like a new disease no one could name.
Their eyes strained to understand
the English-only directions glued to the wall.
Melodic intonations reminded me of my pueblo,
Aguas Buenas.

I didn't want to help.
I didn't want to translate.
I didn't want.

Our eyes met
as I hid my face behind the pages
of Judith Ortiz Cofer's *Latin Deli.*
But it was too late.
Their eyes told me their story:
working in the fields for $50 a week,
picking tomatoes that ended up
in the salads of four star restaurants,
coming home to the one room they all lived in,
the last name they shared—Santiza.

Eyes dark as my grandfather's,
bronze skin like my grandmother's grandfather
who she called El Indio,

lost like me when I was four in kindergarten,
unable to understand the words coming out of Mrs. Farrell's mouth.

I prayed for someone else's humanitarianism
but not mine.
I wished for blonde hair, white skin,
blue eyes, an accentless face.

I thought about the Ivy League diploma
hanging on my living room wall
and the naked walls of the Santiza brothers.

I didn't want to help.
I didn't want to translate.
I didn't want.
As I watched the brothers
ask a stranger: *"¿Habla español?"*

A Poem for the Professors Who Say There is No Place for Bilingualism in Poetry

That afternoon,
as he took the last drag of his cigarette
and moved onto the next topic,
all of the Spanish words
angrily rose from my stanzas.
Scratched their accents and tildes
dubious at what they heard.

They yelled for revolution,
demanded protests and marches.
They held nightly meetings on my desk,
surrounded around a dictionary underneath a poster
of Zapata and Che.

The "ñ's" led discussions
on military tactics and guerilla warfare
as the double "r's" screamed,
"We should have stayed in Neruda's pages!
As least there we were considered genius."

Where did they belong?
What was this thing called "place" and
why couldn't all words exist there?

News spread of the old men who deny words of "place,"
as different languages held caucuses asking questions:
Where do words with accents, tildes, and apostrophes
go when they are shunned from the page and mouth?
If English is not your first but your second or third,
why is it permitted to cut in line?
The French letters wondered
where Eliot fit in this monolinguistic theory:
"Hypocrite lecteur! – mon semblable, - mon frère!"
the Italians wondered about the Cantos:
"Te caveró le budella."

All the words organized and packed their bags,
traveled through deserts and mountains.
Founded their own place
where the old men are prohibited
from issuing prohibitions.

The Other Latina

Contrary to what you hear,
I am not from Iowa.
My life began on a colonized island
and continued in The Bronx.

Financial aid and food stamps.
I lived in an apartment.
My neighbors were drug dealers, welfare children,
pregnant crack addicts, and alcoholics.

I do not want to participate in coffee house discussions
on how Ezra Pound changed my perspective on life.

I do not hide my accent
when I say my name or *burrito*.
Sometimes I will speak Spanish
even though you do not understand
all of the hums and purrs of my tongue.

I do not own West Side Story
or wish to discuss the sociological impact
of Al Pacino in Scarface.

I read and write respectfully in two languages
but sometimes I stumble and
give birth to a new word.

I do not listen to New Age music
or cover my ears when I hear

the bombastic sounds of hip hop cars
creating earthquakes on Bronx street corners.

My shoulders shake
at the congas and timbales
beaten by the memory of the Africano.

I will not lighten my hair or eyes
to make me look beautiful through your camera lens.

My laughter will never be fabricated
so you can feel better about yourself
when you wake up in my bed in the morning.

My family history will not claim
a non-existent 1/8 European uncle
to explain my café con leche skin.

I check ethnicity boxes because
I want you to know that I exist.

I will teach you a different history
of tree frogs serenading coquí
as the sun sets on their island,
independistas named Rafael Cancel Miranda,
women used as guinea pigs for the FDA,
population control in the form of sterilization.

Take you to unemployment offices
and count how many are waiting for a check or a break,
spend the night on death row and listen to the silent stories.

Where Are You From

From the house
my mother worked two jobs to pay for.
From the hallway where I
heard neighborhood chisme about
Doña Carolina and her heroin addicted son Danny
getting out of jail for the third time.

From the bedroom where I
cried realizing I am one of many.
From history
never taught in high school classrooms.
From books
omitted from required reading lists.
From the church pew
where I contemplated my morality as a number
and legacy as a person.

From San Gabriel River Parkway
where T.V. news reports live.
From an insomniac cement stoop
where lottery tickets are confused with maps of freedom.
From the Ivy League
that reported me their most popular statistic
with a picture of me, a white girl and a black man
on the cover of the catalog.

From the land
cultivated by the Indio

renamed by the European.
From the city of New York
where expression is free
and understanding an option.
From the rooftop
where different tongues resonate
a butterfly's whisper.

From the window
I draw a heart on the condensation
watching it bleed on the pane.

Just Too Much

Over lunch one day
my white step-father told me that according
to my resumé
I was too Latina.

He hmphhed and mmed
as he dipped his waffle fries into white vinegar
the taste reminded him of the Palisades
when he was a boy.
He criticized my course of study,
U.S. Latino Experience.
He said it made me come off as a troublemaker.
In the real world
I would be viewed
as the first
to strike.

I lowered the volume of his voice.
My face remained speechless
as my mind ran through a tirade
with an imaginary figure.
In my mind,
my arguments were full of fervor,
wit, and Spanish curses.
My heart held its own debate.
It ranted, cried, yelled, threw imaginary toys
at the impartial figure she thought she knew.
My eyes wandered towards the
greasy diner mirrors.

My brow wrinkled as
I inspected myself between the spots.
My dark straight hair and all year tan — Taina.
My thin lips and native tongue from
my great-grandmother — the Spaniard.
The wide hips from the African slave.

I turned to him and watched his mouth move
as he stirred his third cup of coffee.
He rambled something about society's perceptions
and how lucky I was to have a non-ethnic name.

No one would ever know that I was Latina
by looking at me.
My physical features were not typical.
I had an edge because
my lack of a Spanish accent
and good command of both languages.

When the check came,
he ordered a piece of
Death by Chocolate Cake.

Response to the Young White Man
who Asked Me If I was Scared
of Being Marginalized as a Poet

As a woman, I am already marginalized as a slut, bitch, baby
    machine, sex toy, not-as-good-as-a-man, secretary material
    only;
As a Latina, I am already marginalized as a maid, statistic
    booster, token, white people hater, second coming of J-Lo,
    hot & spicy, uneducated;
As bilingual, I am already marginalized as a foreigner,
    susceptible to people asking me to translate menus for
    them, speaking English at me believing that I do not
    understand them;

To be placed in the company of Julia de Burgos,
feeding me similes, metaphors
sweet like a papaya,
does not bother me.
So please do marginalize me.

My Cockroach Stalker

As I washed my hands in the public bathroom sink,
a cockroach stopped and stared at me
before it skittered away into one of the stalls.
Next day I walked into the last stall
only to find him again,
watching me,
as if saying: "I know where you live."

Attack of the Brown People

Allegedly the 90s sparked the
Latin Invasion.
Neither Orson Welles or Walter Mercado
could have predicted it.
Eyewitness news testimonies ran rampant all across the U.S.:

"They came down from their spaceships
swiveling their leather bound hips and
practicing their new ESL skills

For years they walked amongst us,
hidden behind fences, aprons, and lunch counters,
spoke quickly and musically to one another
as we listened attentively only for some semblance of our name.

We've seen them before:
T.V., movies, late night talk shows,
PBS specials, music videos, magazines.

They wrote award-winning novels,
painted priceless masterpieces,
fought our wars.

They taught us they had been here
before Columbus,
built temples of worship, created zero, developed
cures and new theories for our universes."

Recent reports speculate
Europe is the next target.

The Return of Charo

In November 2001,
Time magazine announced
the return of Charo.

She rediscovered her
cha-chas, coleta, and coochie-coochies.
Her skimpy, sequined dresses,
bright orange like my great-Aunt Tata's living room in 1973,
were taken out of retirement.

Charo had all a Latin entertainer needed:
big dyed hair, long legs, and pouty lips.
We had seen all of this before
when Iris Chacón scandalized our TV sets
with the first televised thong.

Iris' childbearing hips and large mole
above her lip,
hypnotized Telemundo audiences.

She danced for two minutes
between skits for a variety show
with a feather tail and six male dancers in spandex.

Every little girl watched in amazement
as they purposefully rode their underwear
up their brown asses.
Today those little girls are mothers
with little girls listening to their own

sazón flavored music.
Admiring a new set of recycled Latinas
crossing over the musical border
with billion dollar asses,
covering dark roots with their new blond hair.

They all flaunted their sex and race,
defiantly mixing the two like
Bacardi and cocaine.
As we OD,
wishing Charo and her cha-chas good luck.

Cuando La Dejo

When he left her that humid July afternoon,
her feet barely touched
the marble floor of her mother's living room.

No one spoke his name except
with words like "hijo de la gran puta" or "just like your father"
when the mailman delivered water and electric bills on birthdays.

When he left her she was playing Chutes N' Ladders,
announcing he could not live there anymore.
He promised nothing would change.

Tears rolled down her face
as her fingertips touched her forehead,
the moisture of his last kiss.

After he left weekly visits became monthly,
as daily arguments about money and momma's new friend
disappeared like his nightly tuck-ins and bedtime stories.

The next time they saw each other's faces
womanhood had taken shape of her body.
Vignettes of information interrupted the silence.

She probed his face, the gray hairs, wrinkles on his forehead,
the mirror he took when he left her.

15 Minute Bus Ride

I think of the bills that need to get paid
with my pathetic miniscule stipend

my empty refrigerator and
all the cool 3-for-1 supermarket deals

hope that no one sits next to me
in consideration for my comfort

guess whether the person
in front of me has showered in the last few days

the way I miss my bed
on gray, wet days

how asleep I still smell his cologne
as he dresses for work

think about the snooze button that never works
as I try to fix my hair using my reflection in the window

why my stomach makes those noises
every time I pass by Bub's BBQ

wonder about screaming babies and
the overpopulation crisis on public transport

when I am going to see my mom again
and get that car she promised three years ago

why they trust hungover students
to drive these contraptions

pray that I shut the bathroom door
so that my cat does not play scratching post on the Charmin

dream of the 4:46 bus back
to my 700 square feet of paradise.

El Salsero

Each morning before the sun raises its arms
the aroma of sugarcanes
fill Fernando's lungs.

A black cup of coffee energizes him
as he ties strings around his ankles
preventing passage to curious ants or mosquitoes.

With his machete in his right hand,
Fernando tips his pava with his left,
saluting another Puerto Rican sun,
a soldier and his general.

Fernando cuts la caña.
Through the fields,
he hears the command of la conga,
thunder of los timbales.

Every Saturday night
all of las mujeres at El Bohio wait for
El Salsero's arrival,
walking down from his mountain.

With a pressed burgundy guayabera,
slick brown hair,
and a dimple on his left cheek,
he searches for the music
in women's bodies.

The music injects four beats
in and out of his body,
a musical one night stand with a queue of
anxious daughters, minister's wives,
spinsters, and grandmothers
anticipating their five minutes.

The tick, tick of las claves
gravitate him to the stiletto heels
of a red lipped señorita.

His right hand extends with the intrusion of a piano key
as her body grants him permission.

His left hand glides her body across the dance floor.
Their feet and hips obey
the divine consonance of
trumpets, güiros, panderetas.

With each step,
he turns her like a merry-go-around.

Unfinished Portrait

At night,
The Bronx street corners are Graciela's tiny kingdoms
all the men and women know her as La Dueña.
For fifteen years,
she mastered the arts of disease and money.

Regret came once in the form
of a child who had a roulette choice of fathers.
Luckily for the child,
Graciela threw herself down the stairs
the day she heard the news.

Underneath the skin of men
who never knew her,
Rivera makes love to her,
connecting her eyebrows with his fingertips.

In the lonely morning,
she touches the top of her nose
damning the naked gap,
admiring the beauty of The Broken Column
as she untangles dark braids from her hair.

In Graciela's dreams,
stiletto heels tap
the soft steps of Mexican revolucionarios
marching with paintbrushes as weapons,
while her legs gracefully open
like a ballerina pliéing in front of a mirror.

A Journey for the Mute

Salvador woke up one morning in silence.
His lips opened but only air resonated.
His hand reached into his mouth and
searched for his voice box.

His voice box was
alone,
feeling the loss of its companion
Language.

Language left Salvador.
Questions drove him drunk
with no answers for sobriety.

Salvador tried living without Language.
He communicated with noises,
wrote sonnets for the lonely,
had imaginary conversations with imaginary people.

In his mute travels he searched and searched,
Lifted boulders, dug through graveyards,
hoping to find it sitting, waiting
to be found.
To Salvador
this hide-n-go seek game
had no end.

His life remained still and gray
as he continued on his journey.
Passersby like Don Loco Santana
would ask when was the last time
Salvador remembered seeing his Language.

Salvador's mind rewound to the last night
his mother read him a bedtime story.
She would translate Little Red Hiding Hood.
In her version the hood was rojo, the wolf a lobo,
and the grandmother sounded a lot like Abuelita Consuela,
who died when Salvador was 12.

Just before his body lost the struggle against sleep
he would feel his mother's mouth
kissing his cheek
as she asked God to bless her mijo.
Salvador shrugged off Santana's question
along with his memory.
He cursed his god for truths
and Santana for living up to his name: Loco.

So he walked, reclaiming his mission.
He drew pitiful signs
asking anyone if they had seen his Language.
His reward:
a lifetime of thank you letters.

He received a few replies.
One of them from Reverendo Clemente.

He told Salvador the last time
he saw his Language was at Luzdivina's funeral.
Salvador delivered his mother's eulogy,
bestowing all of her fragrances, graces,
and blessings on the congregation.

She was all he had in this fatherless world.
From her he learned to
cook his own rice and beans,
iron the crispest shirts,
and listen selectively.

She was wise.
She knew why chickens didn't fly and
no other mother on the block could match
the softness of her hair.
She was all for him.

Salvador cried in English that day
as Spanish tears drizzled his mother's casket.
He thanked everyone for coming including
the janitor who collected
the loose petals from the floor.

Reverendo Clemente reminded Salvador
of the weekly Spanish mass.
Always on Sundays at 5pm,
Guiros, tambourines, and guitars were welcome
for those "I-need-to-be-saved-again" moments.

Salvador buried Reverendo Clemente's letter
in the freshest soil
on the sunniest side of the Earth
with hopes that it would grow his mother back to life.

Another letter came from
His best friend Cristóbal.
He last saw Salvador's Language
running out of harm's way
the day they were both stopped by the police
at the mall, who did not believe that they could afford
the brand name clothing they were wearing.
The policeman said
even though one of their relatives made the clothing for
5 cents an hour that gave them no right to wear such things.

When he asked for names,
Salvador became Sal and
Torres became Towers.
Cristóbal could not believe
the perfection of
Salvador's Anglo accent.

They were let off with a stern warning
as Cristóbal whistled Officer Krupke
all the way home.
Cristóbal closed his letter asking
after Salvador's whereabouts.
They have not seen each other since that day.

Salvador felt hopeless
as he looked at the piles of letters.
One name stood out from the pile.
It came from Ms. Paloma,
his kindergarten teacher.
She was gorgeous and the first woman
he ever loved aside from his mother.

Ms. Paloma was married,
a hyphen after her name.
She recalled the first time
she saw Salvador's Language.

He entered her classroom with a note
stapled to his brown polyester vest,
listing all of his allergies to paste, crayons,
toxic water colors, finger paint, and some girls.

She introduced herself
with silence as his response.
She tried it again but this time
with her island grown Spanish.

Salvador smiled with four missing teeth
and a weak hola.
That first day Ms. Paloma was the student.
She learned that he was 5,
just arrived in the U.S. with his mother
from a tiny island off Puerto Rico called Vieques.
There were too many explosions to hear the coquis at night.

Salvador had forgotten about that first day,
the vest, the list written in his mother's perfect handwriting.

His eyes filled with images:
Playing street football with Cristóbal,
Sunday masses with tambourines and
everyone asking weekly penance
for weekly sins, and his Abuelita Consuela's skin,
so wrinkled he swore he could peel it off.

He fell to his knees asking for forgiveness
and salvation.
Tears soaked his face
and the land beneath him.
He prayed for the reincarnation
of his Language.

He begged for its return.
Promised never to allow silence
in exchange for acceptance or denial.
He swore to his god and his mother's god.

Dichos y Refranos of the
Sweet Complaint

In the evening when the last toilet brightens
like Orion's belt of pearls,
Carlos greets the front of his East L.A. door
adding its squeak to his mental to do list.

Biology pages stop turning
as Albert carefully picks Lorca off the shelf
like a newborn presented to its parents.

Beginning their moonlight recitation,
father and son sing the first words of the day:

Never let me lose what I have gained, Carlos starts

*And adorn the branches of your river
with leaves of my estranged autumn,* Albert responds.

Adela's Purse

She marched into the upscale department store
with the passion and smoothness of a *corrido*
as butterflies circled her body,
cooling the fair skin inherited by an absent father.

Holding onto her purse purposefully
like a soldier and his rifle,
curly hair pulled back into two long braids.

She marched to customer service
demonstrating the obvious difference
between her purse and the one
they accused her of stealing.

Apologies nor gift certificates were necessary
as Adela pointed out the irony of the word
patron in patronizing.

605 Strawberries

Sitting in infamous
LA traffic
on the 605
between Ramona and
Valley Boulevard
my eyes drift
to the hunched over people
looking back at me
through strawberry fields
a row of "ñ's"
minus the tildes.

Never rising for a break
they pick the freshest strawberries
later dipped by Beverly Hills chocolatiers,
sliced onto fruit platters,
placed as a garnish next to the entrée.

Scenic views of
80 foot power lines and
lottery billboards with the caption
"your eyes don't deceive you"
loom over the organic
while cars sit and stare
like a patrón waiting
for his quota to be met.

From the first rise of
stock brokers, actors, TV executives
revving their six figure Lamborghinis,
to the vertical stretch of
muscle and bone
massaged by red tinted fingers
amalgamated with the sweetness of fruit
and the salt of commerce
as sustenance and sustenance meet.

City Limits

The sign read welcome to Los Angeles
as I said goodbye,

to the coquito man pushing his cart
on those humid July afternoons

when fire hydrants recreated geysers
with the help of a hollow tin can,

bodegas carrying Cola Champagne,
blasting bachata boleros,

men named Papo throwing wooden dominos
on a table supported by two milk cartons,

street corner viejos reminiscing about their islands,
hoping to return because death and birth begin with her,

heat lamps keeping dollar alcapurrias warm
by sweaty cuchifrito windows,

admiring graffiti memorials on storefronts
paying homage to slain children, Pope John Paul II, and Big Pun,

feel the rhythm of a 6 train caboose
sway me back and forth to sleep,

cheer the Bronx Bombers onto yet another victory series,
jeer a Mets fan for being a Mets fan,

buy a hot dog and a pretzel from the same stand,
hear yo, asshole, and puñeta all in one sentence,

visit the gorillas in the morning,
push my way for a small peak at the Rockefeller tree,

watch the wind encircle the fall leaves
into a tornado frenzy,

silently recite the Our Father when I walk by Ground Zero,
touch snow for the first time all over again.

Acknowledgments

Some of these poems first appeared in the following publications:

Children, Churches, and Daddies: "The Return of Charo"

Falling Star Magazine: "605 Strawberries"

Mija Magazine: "The Other Latina"

The Furnace Review: "Dancing Might Make Her Go Away"

Albion Review: "The Return of Charo," "The White Girl in Her"

*Crate: "My Cockroach Stalker," "15 minute Bus Ride"

Latino Today: "Sonnet for José's Enchiladas," "Attack of the Brown People"

Zwiebook Literary Journal: "The Return of Charo," "The White Girl in Her"

Kennesaw Review: "Tattoo of a Child," "Sonnet for José's Enchiladas"

Harpur Palate: "Nightly Prayer to the Unborn Child"

Chase Park Journal: "Questions for the Young Woman Representing Latinos, Puerto Ricans, and People of Color"

Urban Latino Magazine: "The White Girl in Her"

My deepest gratitude, respect and recognition to the following individuals for their unconditional support and patience, and for taking time out of their lives to help me cultivate my craft and see my dream come to fruition. Thank you, Martín Espada for your guidance, friendship, and poetry; to the entire Gilbert-Espada family (pets included) for opening their home and hearts to me and my family; Helena María Viramontes, you made me believe in the power of the female voice; the University of Massachusetts MFA Program for Poets and Writers, where it all began; and Luis Rodriguez and the Tía Chucha Family for their faith in the voice of my poems. Thank you and love to my mother, Carmen Ivette Garcia, and the entire Garcia/Rivera/Muller clan: from Aguas Buenas to NYC and NJ. To my friends and Hermanas for their humor and cheers: Edison, Ivelisse, Melonie, Andre, Quisaira, Paola, Adrienne, Raquel, Jessica, Cielo, Lily, Angie, and Ashika. Finally, to my Antonio, Sofía, y José, without you there would not be any poetry in my world.

About the Author

Luivette Resto was born in Aguas Buenas, Puerto Rico but proudly raised in The Bronx. She graduated from Cornell University with a BA in English Literature and a minor in U.S. Latino Studies. Later, she earned her MFA in Creative Writing from the University of Massachusetts at Amherst. Her commitment to higher education has her teaching English at Citrus College and Mt. San Antonio College. Her poems have been published in *Latino Today, Mija Magazine, Harpur Palate, The Furnace Review,* and *Falling Star Magazine.* Her poetic influences are Martín Espada, Julia de Burgos, Judith Ortiz Cofer, Pedro Pietri, Dorothy Parker, and Pablo Neruda. Currently, she lives in Glendora, California, with her husband José, and her two children, Antonio and Sofía.